Deadly Defenders

SAMANTHA MONTGOMERIE

Collins

Contents

Chapter 1 Powerful poisons 2

Poison dart frogs – facts 12

Chapter 2 Sticky and slimy traps 14

Meet more slimy animals! 22

Chapter 3 Spectacular spikes 24

Quills and spines 34

Chapter 4 Killer claws 36

Claw comparisons 46

Chapter 5 Shooters and showers 48

Inky getaways 56

Chapter 6 A shocking way to go 58

Glossary 68

About the author 70

Book chat 72

Chapter 1

Powerful poisons

Being able to protect yourself from **predators** is important for animals living in the wild. Animals have adapted unique techniques to warn their predators to stay away.

What better way to get rid of a predator than to poison them? Many animals are able to produce terrifying poisons which help them to stop their attackers.

Poison or venom?
If you bite it and you die, then it's poison. But if it bites you and you die, that's **venom**.

Sinister stingers

Scorpions are small arachnids. But they are still scary for predators that are much larger than them, like foxes, rats, owls and frogs. Tiny scorpions use their venom to cause serious harm to their predators.

What are arachnids?

Arachnids have eight legs, two body parts and no wings. Arachnids include spiders, scorpions and ticks.

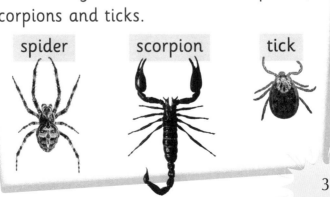

spider   scorpion   tick

3

Scorpions have an abdomen that curls up at the end like a tail. This is called a telson. It has a sharp hollow stinger at the end to inject venom. Scorpions squeeze their venom through the stinger.

When a scorpion injects another animal with venom, something amazing happens!

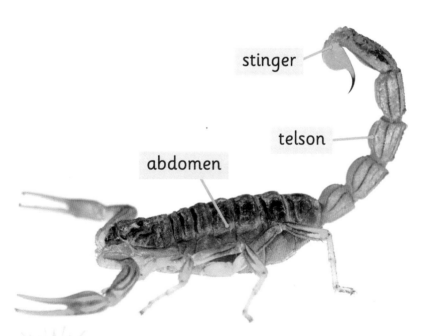

stinger

telson

abdomen

The venom makes it impossible for the animal's brain to tell its body what to do. The animal can't move – and the scorpion can seize the chance to escape.

Scorpion venom has a unique mix of chemicals. Some of the chemicals poison **mammals**, which are the main predators of scorpions. Other chemicals poison insects, so that scorpions can eat the insects!

scorpion stinging a millipede

Exploding ants

Another way to stop predators is to set off a bomb. Some insects make a bomb using their **toxic** insides!

Malaysian exploding ants can turn themselves into bombs like this. They do this to protect other ants in their nests. For ants, the needs of the group are more important than their own needs.

Exploding ants have a body part like a bag inside them, called a **sac**. This is filled with a sticky liquid. When predators appear, ants will angle their backsides towards the predators. The ants flex their stomachs hard, and send out a shower of toxic liquid over the predators. The predators get stuck in the toxic mess and die.

The exploding ants then die too, but at least the rest of the ants are now safe.

Fact!
Scientists say the explosive **toxin** smells like curry!

A venomous primate

With their adorable large eyes and fluffy fur, slow lorises are one of the cutest **primates** in the world. Even so, you should be wary. These animals have some unique ways of protecting themselves.

Slow lorises are the only primates with a venomous bite. They don't produce the venom in their mouth, but under their elbows! A patch on their elbows produces special oil. When slow lorises are attacked, they quickly lick the oil. The oil mixes with the spit in their mouth and turns it into venom. This gets onto their teeth, so they can poison their predators with a nasty bite.

Slow loris parents also lick the heads of their babies, to coat them in venom. This protects the babies by making them poisonous to predators.

Deadly skin

Not all animals can make their own toxins. Poison dart frogs get toxins from eating other animals! These frogs eat toxic ants, beetles and millipedes, and store up the toxins in their skin. When predators touch these frogs, the poison enters the predators' bodies.

Many animals use bright colours as a warning to keep predators away. Poison dart frogs have brightly coloured skins so that they stand out in the rainforest. Their colours act as a warning to predators, telling them to keep away.

How did poison dart frogs get their name? Hunters from South America used to cover their blow darts with toxins from the frogs' skin.

blow dart used in hunting

11

Poison dart frogs – facts

There are more than 100 **species**.

The brighter their colour, the more toxic the frogs.

They live in rainforests in South and Central America.

One golden poison dart frog has enough toxin to kill over ten people.

Golden poison dart frogs are the most toxic. Their toxin can be so strong that it can instantly stop a human heart.

The toxins are only harmful to humans if we eat them.

a golden poison dart frog

Chapter 2

Sticky and slimy traps

Capturing predators in a sticky trap is a great technique. Many animals can make sticky substances to keep their predators away or trap them.

Vomiting birds

Vomiting over other animals is sure to stop an attack. Northern fulmars are birds that use this technique to stop other birds trying to take over their nests.

Northern fulmars begin with a warning to their attacker. They lunge forward with a wide-open beak, squawking loudly.

If the attacker doesn't back down, fulmars try their next trick.

Fulmars have a bright-coloured, stinky oil in their stomach. They can vomit this oil up to 1.5 metres. This foul-smelling oil comes from the fulmars' diet, including fish and squid. The grotesque stench makes predators like foxes run away.

If other birds attack northern fulmars, the vomit sticks the attackers' feathers together, making flying and swimming difficult.

Fact!
The name 'fulmar' translates as 'foul gull'.

Sensational slime

Hagfish are some of the slimiest animals on Earth. They use slime to protect themselves.

Hagfish have around 100 slime **glands** on each side of their bodies. These glands are filled with a thick slimy substance called mucus, and strong silk-like fibres. When hagfish are attacked, the slime in their glands is squeezed out. When the slime hits the water, it expands to 10,000 times its original size! Hagfish can create litres of slime at a time.

Hagfish usually grow up to 50 centimetres long.

Although the slime is incredibly soft, the silk-like fibres make it very strong. Because of this, the slime can cling to predators such as sharks, making it difficult for them to breathe. While their predators are trapped in the slime, the hagfish can make a quick escape to safety.

When hagfish need to escape from their own slime, they tie themselves into a knot and then slither back out of the knot. This rubs the slime off their bodies.

hagfish slime

Tangled in guts

Black sea cucumbers have found a good way to deceive their predators.

They may look harmless, but predators need to be wary. They might find themselves entangled in the sea cucumbers' guts! When attacked, sea cucumbers will shoot out sticky threads from their bottoms. The threads look like fine, sticky noodles, but they are part of the sea cucumbers' guts. The threads tangle up predators, such as crabs, and stop them from attacking.

When they are safe from attackers,
the victorious sea cucumbers will crawl away.

Amazingly, sea cucumbers can regrow their
lost guts! It takes 15 days. During this
time, they are at risk from predators.
But after that, they are armed and ready for
the attack. Due to their **elastic** bodies, sea
cucumbers can stretch out. This lets them
squeeze through gaps in rocks, to hide and
keep themselves safe.

a black sea cucumber
with its sticky threads

Frog glue

Some frogs use sticky substances to protect themselves.

Holy cross frogs have an interesting way to stop predators. There are glands in their skin filled with a glue-like substance. If predators touch these frogs, they will receive a sticky surprise. The gluey substance will ooze out of the frogs' glands and the predators may find themselves stuck.
If the predators try to take a bite of the frogs, they'll get a mouth full of goo.

a holy cross frog with gravel on its sticky skin

Tomato frogs use their sticky skin in a similar way. When under attack, they release a strong sticky substance that covers their body. If a predator tries to bite them, the glue sticks fast to the predator's skin. It numbs the predator's nose and mouth and makes it hard to breathe. This experience is scary for the predator and causes them to drop the frog. This technique helps the small frogs to ward off their much larger predators.

Meet more slimy animals!

Snails use slime in two ways! It helps them slide smoothly, and it also helps them stick to surfaces.

Parrotfish make a slime cocoon around them to keep safe from predators at night.

Some eels use slime to help cement their sandy holes closed to keep themselves safe.

Chapter 3

Spectacular spikes

Spikes can be useful to help animals protect themselves from even the strongest attackers.

There are some unique **marine** and land animals that use their spikes to defend themselves.

Nasty needles

One look at African crested porcupines is enough to put off anyone from approaching them! They are covered in sharp **quills** that grow up to 30 centimetres long!

When they are under threat, porcupines defend themselves by lifting their quills up high.

The quills are hollow, and when porcupines
shake them, they make a rattling sound
like a rattlesnake. This warns any predators
to stay away.

The long quills along the head, neck
and back of crested porcupines stand
up like a crest. This is how they received
their name.

African crested porcupine

African crested porcupines' sharpest quills are
on their back and bottom. Therefore, they
charge backwards at predators with their
quivering quills raised. Then they ram their
quills into the predator. The quills drop out
easily, leaving spines stuck in the predator.
The spikes are very sharp and difficult to
pull out.

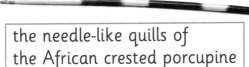

the needle-like quills of
the African crested porcupine

Porcupines rub their quills in mud and
poo, which means the quills carry a lot
of germs. As a result, they can cause
serious infection. Even ferocious lions and
hyenas are wary of porcupines, as an injury
from porcupines' quills can mean death!

Can you see
the porcupine
quills on
this lion?

Hidden spikes

The pufferfish is an unusual marine animal with a sharp set of spikes ready to attack predators. However, they always keep their spikes hidden away until they are needed. Pufferfish have spines which lie flat on their body. When threatened, they use a clever technique to puff up and pop the spines out.

To puff themselves out, these unique fish take huge gulps of water. Muscles in their mouth work like a pump to push the water into their stomach. This technique allows pufferfish to expand like a water balloon. They get very round!

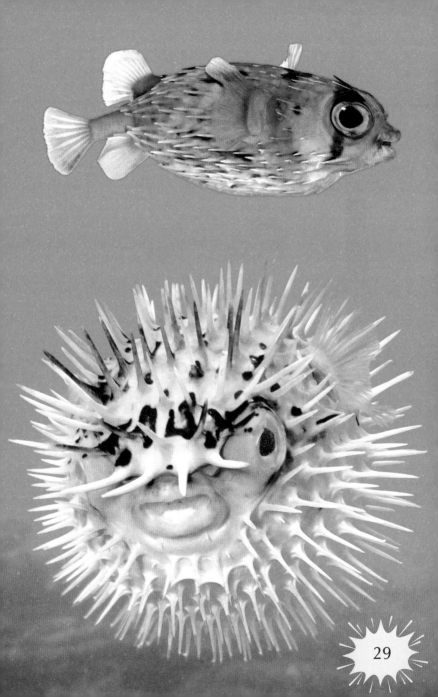

It only takes seconds for pufferfish to triple in size. Their spines pop out and point straight out of their bodies, ready to scare off attackers. Pufferfish also have toxins in their bodies. If animals do eat pufferfish, they swallow these toxins. Predators could die within three minutes of eating the fish. One pufferfish can produce enough toxin to kill 30 humans.

The only marine animals who can swallow pufferfish without dying are sharks. But pufferfish can use their toxic spines to ward off all their other predators!

Fact!

Although pufferfish are very poisonous, some people still choose to eat them. Highly trained chefs have a special technique for preparing the fish. They get rid of almost all the poison. It's an unusual experience to eat pufferfish – it makes your mouth go numb and tingly!

fugu – a dish made from raw pufferfish, sometimes eaten in Japan

Dangerous ribs

Spanish ribbed newts can make spikes from their own bones. These tiny creatures turn their own ribs into spears to warn off any predators. They have eight to ten bumps down each side of their bodies. These are called tubercles, and look like small warts.

Spanish ribbed newt

Tubercles run down both sides of their bodies.

When they are under threat, the newts will arch their backs, pushing their ribs through the bumps. The ribs make holes in their skin, and stick out through the holes, creating a spiky weapon.

The sharp spikes combine with a toxin from their skin. These little creatures can now cause serious damage. When predators try to eat these newts, they also end up eating the toxin. This can cause severe pain or even death.

Quills and spines

There are lots of animals with quills and spines. Here are some ...

hedgehog

Fact: Hedgehogs have around 5,000 spines. They are also naturally **immune** to snake venom!

echidna

Fact: Echidnas and platypuses are the only egg laying mammals!

North American porcupine

Fact: Baby porcupines have very soft quills when they are born. These harden within a few days.

sea urchin

Fact: Sea urchins are sometimes called sea hedgehogs. Their spines range from three to 30 centimetres long!

Chapter 4

Killer claws

What do you picture when you think of clawed animals? Maybe you think of bears or tigers, with fearsome fangs and claws at the ready. But it may surprise you to know that clawed creatures come in all shapes and sizes. Lots of animals, big and small, use their claws to defend themselves from attackers.

Hidden weaponry

Platypuses have sharp spikes called spurs on their rear legs. These spurs are loaded with venom. Platypuses usually keep their spurs flat until they need to use them.

a platypus spur hidden on the inside of their back legs

When they need to protect themselves, platypuses can stick their spurs out at an angle, ready for use. Platypuses use a fighting technique where they wrap their hind legs around their enemy. The platypuses then kick hard, driving their spurs into their enemies' flesh.

The platypuses' venom is made in glands near the spurs. The venom is very painful and can make the platypuses' victims freeze for a while. This guarantees that the platypuses can escape.

Fact!
Platypuses are one of only a few venomous mammals in the world.

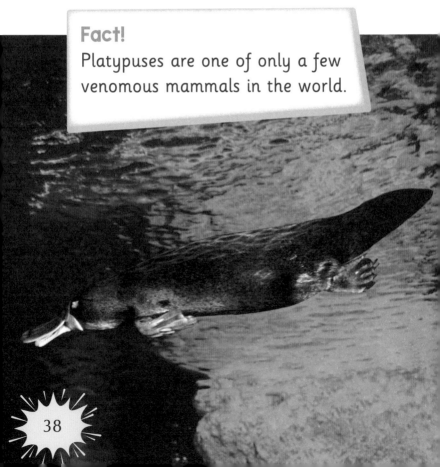

A killer kick

Look at this cassowary. You might think its helmet-like crown is its best defence – but don't be deceived!

In fact, cassowaries' claws are their most effective weapon. The longest claw is on the inner of their three toes, and it can grow up to an impressive 13 centimetres long. The claws are also very sharp. This makes them useful when cassowaries need to protect themselves from large enemies.

long claw

Cassowaries' long legs make them powerful jumpers. When threatened, cassowaries can jump two metres into the air. This allows them to pounce on large predators such as crocodiles. Cassowaries kick in a forward and downward direction, using their dagger-like claws. This can cause serious damage to their predators.

Leaping cassowaries can jump so high that they can kick an adult human in the chest.

Because they weigh up to 40 kilograms, there's a lot of power behind cassowaries' kicks! These clever birds use their bodies to keep themselves out of danger when their predators attack.

Cassowaries are the world's most dangerous birds.

World champion claws

The title of the world's largest claws goes to giant armadillos. They have a long central claw on both of their front feet that can grow up to 20 centimetres long. These impressive claws make seriously good digging tools. They help armadillos to tear up termite mounds to find food. However, the claws also make a useful weapon.

a giant armadillo

Unlike most armadillos, giant armadillos can't roll into a ball for protection. Instead, when cornered by a predator, giant armadillos use their claws to guard themselves. Giant armadillos warn their predators by rising up on their hind legs, using their tails to balance. They extend their long claws and get ready to attack.

A giant armadillo in its attack stance.

Fact!
Giant armadillos also have more teeth than any other mammal. They have 100!

43

Hairy frogs

Hairy frogs have found a unique way of protecting themselves. They can break their own bones to make claws. Due to this grotesque behaviour, they are often called 'horror frogs'.

Fact!

Hairy frogs get their name due to the hair-like structures that can grow on the body and thighs of the male frogs.

Horror frogs have a special muscle attached to their back leg bones. When attacked, they squeeze the muscle. This pulls the bone down, snapping it. The broken end of the bone then sticks out like a claw.

This turns the feet of the hairy frogs into ghastly weapons. A few kicks stop their enemies from attacking.

After the attack, the bone claws move back into place. The toe wounds heal over, ready to use them next time.

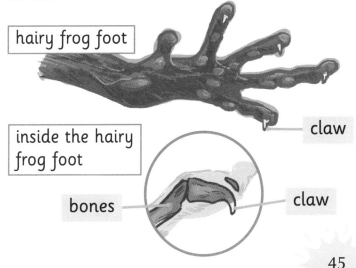

hairy frog foot

inside the hairy frog foot

claw

claw

bones

Claw comparisons

fox 2 centimetres

lion 4 centimetres

Komodo dragon 5 centimetres

harpy eagle 10 centimetres

cassowary 13 centimetres

giant armadillo 20 centimetres

Chapter 5

Shooters and showers

Some animals can spit, squirt and spray to
defend themselves in unusual ways.
Even animals that look harmless,
like shrimps, can sometimes surprise
their enemies.

A toxic spit shower

What could be more ghastly than being
spat at with a stream of toxic spit?
Mozambique spitting cobras are some
of the cleverest animals on the planet.
Other snakes use their fangs to inject venom
into their **prey**. Mozambique spitting cobras
use their fangs to spray venom.

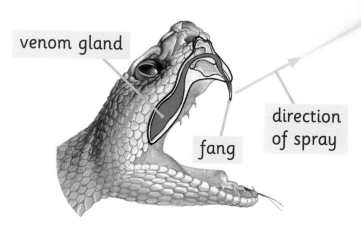

venom gland

fang

direction of spray

Mozambique spitting cobras have special venom glands at the back of their mouths. Small holes at the front of their fangs allow the venom to flow through. Unlike other cobras, the holes in Mozambique spitting cobras' fangs are at an angle. This gives them even more chances of hitting their predators with their toxic spit. They can even spit while still lying on the ground.

Mozambique spitting cobras are clever in their aim. By changing the angle of their jaws, they can direct their venomous spray straight into the eyes of their predators.

They can also successfully hit their target from a long distance away. Their spit can travel for more than two metres! This is an excellent technique for fighting off predators without having to get too close to them.

When toxins from the cobras' spit get into their victims' eyes, it's very painful. It can even cause their victims to go blind. While the predators have lost their vision, Mozambique spitting cobras have time to slither away.

a Mozambique spitting cobra

Bubble bullets

There are some clever shooters on the seabed who can stun predators with a single shot. Pistol shrimps may deceive you with their tiny size, growing to just three to five centimetres long.

However, they're armed with a powerful weapon, because one of their claws is enormous! This claw can grow up to half the size of their body. They use this claw like a gun, firing out bubble bullets to stun their predators.

a full-grown pistol shrimp

The pistol shrimps open their claw and then slam it shut so fast that a bubble shoots out. The bubble travels fast, at around 100 kilometres an hour, hurtling towards its target. When the bubble pops, it makes a sound louder than a gun being fired. The bubble is also super-hot — four times hotter than lava. The whole thing happens within a fraction of a second.

Fact!
Divers say that when lots of pistol shrimps fire bubbles at once, it sounds like a hundred people cracking their knuckles!

Clouds of poo

Most of us wouldn't race towards our prey if they created a large cloud of poo around us. That's what pygmy sperm whales do! It's a technique that guarantees the whales a quick escape when they're chased by predators.

Pygmy sperm whales are only 1.2 metres long, not much larger than a dolphin. They are very slow creatures and often **bask** in the sunlight. This makes pygmy whales easy for their predators to spot.

Unlike bigger whales, these little whales need something to keep them safe.

It might sound strange, but large clouds of poo are their solution.

Remember the gulls that used vomit to scare off predators? Well, these ingenious whales use a similar technique. Pygmy sperm whales have a sac filled with 12 litres of dark liquid in their guts. When they feel threatened by predators such as sharks, they release this into the water. The dark reddish-brown poo makes a massive cloud behind them. This can spread over 100 metres – that's the size of four tennis courts. The dark cloud protects the whales and allows them to escape.

Fact!
The Japanese name for pygmy sperm whales translates as "firecracker whale" due to the clouds of colour they explode into the water.

Sperm whale releasing
a poo cloud so predators
can't see it.

Inky getaways

Octopuses and squids squirt ink to escape from predators. This is called 'defensive inking'.

The ink also warns other octopuses that a predator is close.

Some octopuses make ink clouds the same size as them, then dart away. This inky 'shadow' confuses predators.

Fire squids squirt out a glowing light that looks like a shower of sparks!

Chapter 6

A shocking way to go

There are some shocking underwater creatures that use electric energy to keep them safe. Different animals vary in how they use electricity to scare away predators.

High voltage eels

Electric eels get their name from their ability to give an electric shock. These clever creatures use electricity to find their way, find their prey and knock back their predators.

Electric eels make their electricity through special cells in their bodies. Each eel has 6,000 of these cells. These cells are arranged like stacks of batteries. They provide a unique way for the eels to experience their watery world.

Instead of using their eyes, the eels give out a weak electric signal to find their way around. The signals work like feelers, scanning the environment to see what's nearby.

an electric eel

If they detect a predator, electric eels will send out a high-voltage shock. This technique shocks the predator and stuns it so that it can't move. For larger predators, electric eels sometimes wrap themselves around the animal, which doubles the strength of the electric shock. The predators quickly get exhausted and the eels can escape.

Electric eels can produce an electrical charge as high as 600 volts – that's five times as strong as an electrical socket in your house! The shock is so powerful that it could knock a horse off its feet.

Fact!
A volt is a measure of how strong a current of electricity is.

electric eels

Fact!
Electric eels are technically not eels at all, but a sort of fish.

Electric eels can produce shocks for up to an hour. These eels can also leap from the water to deliver shocks to animals that pose a threat.

While their shocks can't kill humans, people can still receive a large jolt. Victims have explained that it feels like running into an electric fence.

Electric rays

Some other fish, like rays, have the ability to make electrical energy. Electric rays are large, flat fish. They produce electricity in a similar way to electric eels. The rays have two glands on the sides of their heads, with electricity-producing cells. The level of voltage these creatures produce varies depending on the number of electricity cells they have. Torpedo rays can stun predators with a 50-volt shock.

a torpedo ray

An ancient wonder

Stories about the electrical energy of rays go right back to the ancient Greeks. A zap from electric rays can cause numbness, so the Greeks referred to them as "numbfish". They also applied electric rays to their bodies to treat severe headaches. They even used them to numb the pain of patients in operations.

an electric torpedo ray

Electric catfish can grow to more than a metre in length. The strength of their shock depends on their size. Larger fish can produce 450 volts – enough to stun an adult human. They can produce a shock that lasts for up to 30 seconds. Electric catfish use their energy to defend their territory, scaring away predators.

Fact!
The long whiskers on a catfish are called barbels. These help them to smell and taste.

Electric catfish are shown in ancient
Egyptian pictures dating back 5,000 years.

ancient Egyptian
fishing scene

Their name in the ancient Egyptian language translates as "he who has saved many lives in the sea". This is because catfish often shocked people while they were fishing. They then dropped their fish back into the sea, and the fish swam away. The catfish therefore saved the lives of many other fish who were caught in the net!

Conclusion

Animals have a range of incredible tricks to keep themselves alive in the wild. They can use their spikes, spit, stingers and claws to stop the most ferocious of predators. They can use their bodies in amazing ways to become victorious deadly defenders.

Which defender amazed you most?

Glossary

bask relax in the sunshine and enjoy the heat

elastic stretchy

glands parts of an animal's body that make things such as sweat, tears and poison

immune not harmed by

mammals all animals that have hair and feed their babies with milk (including humans)

marine found in the sea

predators animals that hunt other animals for food

prey an animal that is hunted by other animals for food

primates mammals such as monkeys
and apes

quills special kinds of hairs which grow as
sharp as needles

sac a bag-shaped body part that
contains liquid

species a group of animals similar to
each other

toxic poisonous

toxin a poisonous substance that can
harm or kill living things

venom a poisonous fluid in the bite or
sting of some animals

About the author

Why did you want to be an author?

I have always loved great stories. As a child, I read lots of books. I would sometimes get into trouble for reading and not going to sleep when I was supposed to! I wanted to be an author so that I could enjoy writing great stories like the ones I loved to read.

Samantha Montgomerie

What's the best thing about writing?

The best thing about writing is finding out new and interesting things – like the wonderful animal defences in this book! Then, spending days finding just the right words to tell you all about them. I also love to write imaginative stories that take me to new places with fun characters I have created.

Why did you want to write this book?

Animals are amazing! I love reading about all the interesting creatures around the world. Some of my most-loved books are animal reference books with pages on different animals. Animals are so good at using their bodies to do great things, like fending off predators. And who wouldn't want to write about dagger-like claws and toxic spit?

How do you research a book like this?

I usually start at my local library and find the best books I can about my topic. I spend hours reading and making lots of notes in my notebooks. Then I will look up information on the internet where experts share what they know. This includes reading articles and watching videos. For every fact I find, I check it across several sources.

What do you hope readers will get from the book?

I hope readers will find out new things about these interesting animals and the truly amazing ways they defend themselves. Maybe they will even meet some animals they have not heard about before. I also really hope it will inspire them to read more books about animals.

Have you ever seen an animal defend themselves?

When I was having a picnic with my family, I got a bee sting on my foot. It was a very clever way for the bee to stop me squishing it! I think I saw it smiling as it flew away ...

What animal would you love to see? Why?

I really want to see a pygmy whale. I love to spend time in the sea and I adore the animals that live there. I love to go snorkelling in the sea to see what I can find. I've seen a humpback whale, a sperm whale and a killer whale. Seeing a pygmy whale would be amazing. But I guess I will keep a safe distance in case it decides to shower me in poo!

Book chat

What did you know about animals defending themselves before you read this book?

What have you learnt from reading this book?

Have you ever seen any of these animals?

Which animal would you most like to see and why?

If you had to describe this book to someone, what would you say?

Which animal do you think has the most interesting defence?

If you could ask the author a question, what would you ask?

What do you think is the best photo in the book? Why do you like it?

What was the most interesting thing you learnt from reading this book?

If you had to give the book a new title, what would you choose?

Do you think this book would make a good TV show? Why or why not?

Which part of
the book did you like
best and why?

Would you recommend
this book?

Book challenge:

Choose any animal and find
out how it defends itself.

Collins

BIG CAT

Published by Collins An imprint of HarperCollins*Publishers*

The News Building	Macken House
1 London Bridge Street	39/40 Mayor Street Upper
London	Dublin 1
SE1 9GF	D01 C9W8
UK	Ireland

© HarperCollins*Publishers* Limited 2024

10 9 8 7 6 5 4 3 2 1

ISBN 978-0-00-868114-2

Download the teaching notes and word cards to accompany this book at: http://littlewandle.org.uk/signupfluency/

Get the latest Collins Big Cat news at
collins.co.uk/collinsbigcat

Author: Samantha Montgomerie
Illustrator: Caitlin O'Dwyer (Astound Illustration Agency)
Publisher: Laura White
Product manager: Caroline Green
Series editor: Charlotte Raby
Development editor: Catherine Baker
Commissioning editor: Suzannah Ditchburn
Project manager: Emily Hooton
Copyeditor: Sally Byford
Proofreader: Catherine Dakin
Cover designer: Sarah Finan
Typesetter: 2Hoots Publishing Services Ltd
Production controller: Katharine Willard

Printed in the UK.

MIX
Paper | Supporting responsible forestry
FSC
www.fsc.org
FSC™ C007454

This book is produced from independently certified FSC™ paper to ensure responsible forest management.

For more information visit: www.harpercollins.co.uk/green

Made with responsibly sourced paper and vegetable ink

Scan to see how we are reducing our environmental impact.

Acknowledgements
The publishers gratefully acknowledge the permission granted to reproduce the copyright material in this book. Every effort has been made to trace copyright holders and to obtain their permission for the use of copyright material. The publishers will gladly receive any information enabling them to rectify any error or omission at the first opportunity.

Front cover & piii Eric Isselee/Shutterstock, piv Michiel de Wit/Shutterstock, p2 Aastels/Shutterstock, p3t WildScapePhotos/Alamy, p3bl Eric Isselee/Shutterstock, p3bc Den Rozhnovsky/Shutterstock, p3br nechaevkon/Shutterstock, p4 jcm32/Shutterstock, p5 Wayan Sumatika/Shutterstock, p7 Minden Pictures/Alamy, p8 Wang LiQiang/Shutterstock, p9 g images.com/Shutterstock, p10 Dirk Ercken/Shutterstock, p11 Renato Granieri/Alamy, p13 Thorsten Spoerlein/Shutterstock, p15 Annelies Leeuw/Alamy, p16 Brandon Cole Marine Photography/Alamy, p17 Ted Small/Alamy, p18 imagebroker.com GmbH & Co. KG/Alamy , p19 José María Barres Manuel/Alamy, p20 Kristian Bell/Shutterstock, p21 Eric Isselee/Shutterstock, p22t Gregorius Bryan/Shutterstock, p22b Sanit Fuangnakhon/Shutterstock, p23t Helmut Corneli/Alamy, p23b MK PhotoVideo/Shutterstock, p25 mariait/Shutterstock, p26 Smiler99/Shutterstock, p27t JethroT/Shutterstock, p27b Tobie Oosthuizen/Shutterstock, p29t Eric Isselee/Shutterstock, p29b Jung Hsuan/Shutterstock, p30 Eric Isselee/Shutterstock, p31 norikko/Shutterstock, p32 Gecko1968/Shutterstock, p33 Vitalii Hulai/Shutterstock, p34t Eric Isselee/Shutterstock, p34b Eric Isselee/Shutterstock, p35t Ultrashock/Shutterstock, p35b photossee/Shutterstock, p37t S_Images.com/Shutterstock, p37b Auscape International Pty Ltd/Alamy, p38 Imagebroker/Alamy Stock Photo, p39 phugunfire/Shutterstock, p40 De Agostini Picture Library/Getty Images, p41 Santonius Santonius Silaban/Alamy, p42 Kevin Schafer/Alamy, p43 Nature Picture Library/Alamy, p44 Paul Starosta/Getty Images, p48 Craig Cordier/Shutterstock, p49 Ekaterina Gerasimchuk/Shutterstock, p50 Stu Porter/Shutterstock, p51 Subphoto.com/Shutterstock, p55 Rob Atherton/Shutterstock, p56 Jeff Rotman/Alamy, p57 Dante Fenolio/Science Photo Library, p59 Minden Pictures/Alamy, p61 tristan tan/Shutterstock, pp62–63 stephan kerkhofs/Shutterstock, p64 Kevin Griffin/Alamy, p65 Nature in Stock/Alamy, p66 Granger Historical Picture Archive/Alamy, back cover spatuletail/Shutterstock.